Sequelae

tanka prose

David C. Rice

Art by Tex Buss

Text copyright by David C. Rice, 2022
Art copyright by Tex Buss, 2022

Just Keep Walking Press, Berkeley, California, 2022
Contact: davidrice13131@gmail.com

ISBN: 978-1-7331154-3-8

For my grandchildren—David

For my girl—Tex

We are donating all proceeds from the sale of this book to the Climate Emergency Fund.

"What will summer be like as temperatures continue to rise? In the carefully vetted formulation of the IPCC (Intergovernmental Panel on Climate Change), many changes in the climate system become larger in direct relation to increasing global warming." In other words, we really don't want to find out. But, unfortunately, we are going to."—Elizabeth Kolbert

". . . Industrial civilization is functionally and inherently unsustainable. It will not—indeed cannot— last forever, and after this way of living is no longer tenable, we would prefer . . .that more of the living planet remain, rather than less."—*Bright Green Lies.* Derrick Jensen, Lierre Keith, & Max Wilbert.

"We are making choices that will affect whether beings thousands of generations from now will be able to be born sound of mind and body. . . The most radical thing any of us can do at this time is to be fully present to what is happening in the world." —Joanna Macy

"[Birds] are our last, best connection to a natural world that is otherwise receding."—Jonathan Franzen

Contents

Introduction

How can we get there from here? How can we re-connect to the earth? Environmental activists demonstrate how we could change direction. Scientists keep telling us what will happen if we don't. Climate fiction writers, poets and visual artists keep showing us what will happen if we don't. Journalists report on the small changes we are making. We are making small changes, but we certainly haven't changed direction yet.

Tanka poetry, a five-line form written in Japan for the past twelve-hundred years, and by English-language poets for about a hundred years, limits the poet's ability to explore the complexities and nuances of our lives, compared to free verse poetry, due to its brevity. Tanka compensate for this, to some degree, by emphasizing the links-and-shifts between the five lines and by crystallizing emotional responses to specific perceptions. Tanka prose, by providing a context for the tanka, also serves to stretch the short poem's reach.

> dawn
> three coyotes watch me
> and a thrush sings
> could be the last century
> —we can't go back

The most popular outdoor recreational activity in the US, by far, is birding. When the front yard persimmon tree is leafless, suet and seed feeders bring sparrows, finches, and an occasional wren into focus within six feet of our dining room window. (No cardinals—I live in California.)

If I move slowly down the walkway, every now and then a bird stays on the feeder and doesn't fly off, as if, anthropomorphically speaking, it trusts me. In our local park, I've walked around juncos feeding on the path and, sometimes, they don't flee back into the brush as I pass. When this happens, I'm grateful, as if we're sharing the earth together, which we are.

Just Human?

Growing Up Is Hard To Do

Is it a developmental given that a society's energy usage increases indefinitely, regardless of the environmental cost? Our relationship with the earth has been stuck at the toddler stage since the industrial revolution began: If I want it, it's mine. If I can take it away from you, it's mine. If it looks like mine, it's mine. We're over-sized toddlers, ripping the earth apart like its wrapping paper and every day's our birthday.

> quail chicks
> scurry after their parents
> we follow
> the gross national product
> up a flim-flam ladder

Circle Time

fires north and south
sun smoke-dark at noon
everyone stay inside
wonder if today
might wake us up

We can't go out today. Too much smoke. Remember the show we watched yesterday about how the earth needs our help? What do you think we should do?

"We could send a spaceship! With a gigantic vacuum cleaner to suck up all the bad air! Whoosh—all gone!"

"We could plant super trees that would eat all the bad air!"

"We could make the President wear solar clothes. If he didn't have any, he'd have to wear pajamas!"

Anyone else? Okay. Thank you so much for sharing. Ask your parents how they're helping the earth.

young couples push strollers
five-year-old soccer girls
do calisthenics . . .
what's the expiration date
of our old normal?

Too Hard To Stop?

Our desire for comfort exponentially multiplied the law of unexpected consequences.

soot from fires
fifty miles away
on the front step railing
a friend hopes
she doesn't become a grandmother

Science hasn't helped us. The drug to curb our addiction to convenience has had limited efficacy in repeated trials.

my grandmother never spoke
of the pogrom
so many ways
to die
prematurely

Where We're Going

    Unlike explorers of old, who had to guess—*terra incognita* . . . dragons?— we've set off on a journey to the end of the earth with accurate maps, and it turns out dragons do exist: our fire-breath is proof.

> noon
> no sun
> we stay in
> turn the lights on
> and the smoke alarm off

How Do We Get There From Here?

We know the route, but our packs are heavy. What can we do without? Empty the packs. Only put back what we absolutely need. Okay, a few conveniences and whims. If too many of us carry too much, we'll travel too slowly, and our water will run out before we get over the pass.

> distant smoke
> drooped shooting stars
> around a mud-rimmed lake
> to get to the mega-drought
> we just need to keep going

Hope Is Not A Plan

If all countries met current *goals*, the likely global temperature increase by 2100 is 1.8 degrees Celsius (range 1.5-2.4).

the wind
blows a leaf
just out of reach
we are free
to keep falling

The predicted temperature rise by 2100 based on current *policies* is 2.7 Celsius (range 2.0 -3.6).

ducks
explode from the marsh
before I see them
we don't move fast enough
to escape ourselves

Range Expansion

Canaries in the arctic? Why not, as the ice retreats? Would that be warning enough that danger is imminent? Maybe not. Our desire not to squelch our desires distorts our vision. Or maybe canaries reaching the arctic is natural, because the consequences of our genetic inability to control ourselves are inevitable.

up on a ridge
migrating swallows
curlicue past
where we're going
is off course

Honor Roll?

Fire-smoke ignores zip codes, bad-to-breathe air and tainted water concentrate in less affluent neighborhoods and, though climate justice advocates protest, there are a thousand ways to say NIMBY. We're all in a mixed flock, but too many of us privilege our own plumage.

kindergarten bird art
—blue jay, goldfinch, cardinal—
we all need to graduate
from the school
of primary colors

QED

Introduction: The changing climate is an "existential threat" to life on earth. We investigated how willing individuals might be to make changes to lower greenhouse gas emissions significantly. *Method*: Internet Questionnaire. *Results*: Life-style changes that would make life more inconvenient are not a high priority. *Conclusion*: Most people want to do what's right but don't want to give up what they have. Further research is needed to discover how to motivate people to break their bad climate habits.

But can the scientific method help? Isn't this an acceptance-of-death problem? Don't too many of us just not want to deprive ourselves too much while we're here—even though we're destroying what keeps us going—because eventually we'll be gone.

> a hawk bursts
> onto the porch and seizes
> a jay on the rail
> the apex predator
> never stops preying

Conundrum

As consumers—seventy percent of the economy— we purchase pizza and movies-on-demand to distract us from the runaway climate news. As long as we don't stop, we won't feel too badly.

> the hawk arrives
> catches another siskin
> we don't need
> to buy stuff
> to survive

Can art help us help the earth?

> on a window ledge
> a long-legged shorebird
> as they disappear
> we'll carve, sculpt, paint
> more

Tech Support?

How maintain our civilization at the level to which we have become accustomed, given our energy problem? Theoretically, it's a simple matter of supply and demand, and the tech wizards are currently at work turning dross into eco-gold: lab-grown "beef," super-battery storage, carbon-sequestering gizmos.

Let's assume battery-powered long-distance airplanes and ignore the scarcity-of-essential-rare-minerals problem. Let's say they can even genetically engineer cells to take carbon dioxide out of the air in a way that makes financial sense, and that we will sign up for the recurring monthly charges when their investors demand stock-splits, disguised as flavored earth-savers.

Well, you can go online and bet on what the price of carbon emissions will be in the future. I don't want to bet against us but don't much like the odds we'll win before the climate clock strikes midnight.

> that 1990's photo
> burnt trees on the ridge
> above the trail
> a foretelling
> I didn't believe back then

Zero-Point Plan

We talk about renewing our commitment to the earth, but it's hard to adopt a more climate-friendly life-style on our own. We need political help. Politicians won't lead unless they think we'll follow, though, and we are change-adverse. When the rivers overflow their banks, politicians use emergency funding. Sometimes they talk about long-term plans—Rachel Carson bless them—but they rarely talk about how we discard too much stuff and use too much to start with. The way we exploit the earth is an ongoing spirit-sink, but politicians are not going to lead us out of the temptation of accumulation unless we make them.

> I put my nose
> in a blooming honeysuckle
> too many leaders pay
> to get out
> of this basic training

Lost and Found?

Native cultures have lived with the earth for millennia and have not tried to conquer it. Not sure their tightly-stitched community approach is scalable to our mammoth human population and global economy. Recently, at the President's request, all the Secretaries submitted reports of how climate change will affect their purview: Agriculture—threats to food supply; Defense—more international conflicts; Transportation—more roads and tunnels flooded. Recommended solutions included use less energy, improve supply chains, and protect people from rising temperatures.

What about more fundamental solutions? What about a Department of Native American Wisdom to give a national platform for its Secretary to both nudge us into respecting the earth and also propose and enforce regulations that will stop us from sweeping so much of what keeps us alive into an industrial dustbin?

> huge decline
> in bird populations
> I need to do more
> than keep our cats
> indoors

Next Court Date In Six Months

    At the preliminary hearing, the Supreme Gaia council ordered all adults to wear smart phones, programmed to measure how much we're doing to leave the oil in the ground. Industry argued such monitoring was unnecessary.

        sheltering-in-place
        we loosened the noose
        cinched
        around the earth's neck
        watched the biosphere breathe again

The granddaughters demurred.

        the risk
        of green-to-smog recidivism
        is higher than a hawk's flight
        they'll just re-attach
        the jesses to our hopes.

Room For Improvement

If we were to change our climate course, who would steer? The wealthiest five-percent, who use thirty-five percent of the carbon, are on cruise control. Those who lack resources are just trying to stay on the road. Can those of us in the middle grab the wheel and turn us off the super-sized highway?

> a woodpecker hammers
> but that telephone pole
> is no longer a tree
> how do we drill
> beneath our daily routines?

On The Road

a blue sky
meadowlark-sparrow-song day
when the climate siren
is silent
feels like we're all clear

Two weeks before the UN climate summit, our Senate is evenly divided: shall we save the earth or let it go? Business sees the President's plan for reducing greenhouse gases as revolutionary, not in a we're-really-gonna-do-it, tea-in-the-harbor way, but in a not transitional-enough way. In other words, business is advising the President to scale back his plan and go slower.

Without the political will and business support, we'll continue to inch along as the fires and floods speed past us.

those butterflies
who arrive
where they've never been . . .
we need to break out
of our cocoons

Not On The Wagon Yet

Listened to Greta T., on YouTube, talking about the inadequacy of the politicians' responses to the climate crisis. After one week, 45K viewers, 2K likes, 1.4K dislikes. There's the nub. Too many people want to respond as if we have a problem, not a crisis, and want incremental solutions, which don't solve crises.

Greta T. is not anonymous, of course, but there are millions of anonymous people committed to following a real crisis management program, if only our leaders would implement one. Alas, there are millions more who still aren't in recovery. What it will take for a lot more of us to hit bottom, and admit the comfort of business-as-usual has become unsustainable, is the great mystery.

> a thrush
> slings its song
> through the redwoods
> if only everyone
> could catch it

No Exit?

Read another book: a gazillion fewer mono-crops and a gazillion more trees would lead us out of our industrial malaise. Over time, ever-increasing tons of carbon would be sequestered, temperatures would stop rising, and we all could chill.Oh, and leave most of the remaining oil, gas, and coal in the ground.

But there's no breadcrumb-trail to follow, and we keep scampering into dead ends. Our maze is huge—and expanding.

If only we could find the way out.

> young climate activists
> accuse our leaders
> of *blah, blah, blah*
> coward-belly yellow and steel blue
> don't mix to forest green

Not Too Big To Fail

Sign in the campground: *Leave no crumbs.* Jays and ravens eat them, produce more jays and ravens, who then eat endangered Marbled Murrelets.

no-moon-no-lights night sky
my granddaughter says
we're so small
here on earth
we're giants

Ninety-six percent of the historic redwoods logged. Monetized. We now see that as excessive. Should we have stopped at four percent? Fifty percent? Will we mine ninety-six percent of the coal, oil, and natural gas and then create national parks to protect the rest?

redwood hike
—a twelve-foot diameter titan—
membership
in the save-the-earth club
requires photo id

It *Is* All About Us

We all have something different to say about the changing climate. Yes, there are the deniers and minimizers, but also the doom-sayers, the exasperated, and the hopeful. What kind of climate-responder are you, as we all mosey toward uninhabitability?

"It's like two kids, each wearing an oxygen mask, walking over scorched earth, and the father is handing each kid their inheritance: a bag of money."

"It's about money and class. We could farm sustainably, and people could still eat some beef. It would be harder and would cost more, but agribiz doesn't want to do that and governments don't want to make them do it."

"If every couple had zero or one child, we could reduce the earth's population to a more manageable level in four generations, which would help a lot, but that won't happen."

> no more shrikes
> on our annual bird count
> I've got to let go
> of my puny lifetime
> and think geologic

Beneficiaries?

We value the present over the future, aren't motivated by fear, exhortation, information, or extrinsic rewards, and beliefs override facts. It's hard to avoid the conclusion that we are going to keep using too much unsustainable energy and keep making life harder for ourselves and every other species.

> chainsaw roar
> an arborist thins
> introduced eucs
> we're the invasive species
> who can't manage itself

Trying to figure out how to help, I always end up on the same dead-end path at the edge of a cliff. The industrial revolutionaries mistook invention for unadulterated progress. It's likely to be decades before the climatic apocalypse peaks. There's still time to mitigate. We won't go extinct, but lots of us will likely die, and living will be much more difficult for those who don't.

> I sacrifice some
> — you do, too—
> not enough
> for our great-grandchildren
> to forgive us

Progress Interrupted

Variolation before we knew how vaccines worked. Oil-gas-coal energy before we understood how greenhouse gases work.

We listened when biologists figured out our immune system, but when climatologists, writers, movie directors, artists, and poets tell us, as they have for the last eighty years, that we need to emit fewer greenhouse gases, we hesitate. We quibble. As we head toward a climate tipping point where the changes become irreversible, will we reach a psychological tipping point and plunge into green before it's too late?

> an empty store
> with the solar system sketched
> on its window
> we will not be moving
> to outer space

Mandatory Mediation?

Agreed Upon Facts: A day-long deluge, unprecedented at that time of year, roiled the river into a Class V rapids. The protesters' boats, *Short-term Greed* and *Fiddlin' While We Sink*, capsized. You, Officer Grimrod, waited until the next day to order helicopter reconnaissance.

Disputed Facts: Their relatives said you should have, and could have, prioritized their search and rescue. You claimed the economy was underwater, you were in meetings all afternoon, and that people who go into the wilderness assume full responsibility for any risks they take.

> my grandson
> catches and releases
> a trout too small to keep
> we can't find
> what we've already lost

Letter From The Future

Couldn't you have taken less and left more? I mean your ancestors gave you a functioning planet. You had roses and redwoods, robins and roadrunners. It's hard to accept so many of you are gone, and that you took so many others with you.

> dusk
> turns to dark
> the last robin calls
> our flashlights reveal
> how little we see

Daydream

Suppose we made peace with the earth.

       preteen grandkids
       mesmerized
       by the no-longer-endangered lemurs
       wouldn't ask why
       we chopped their forests down

Just Human?

Extinction is geologically common, whether meteor-crunched or self-induced.

> drip . . . drip . . .
> descendants, please know,
> before you disappear
> we found the leak
> just couldn't stop it

Can we make an evolutionary leap back into the web of life we thought we didn't need?

> optometry exam—
> we're near-sighted
> can't read the last line
> on the chart . . .
> *hubris.*

Suppose our population just crashes by ten percent and only a billion of us have to relocate . . .

> my granddaughter shows me
> a teen's YouTube
> smoke blackens green fields
> and an adult says
> *sorry*

Eco-Grief

I wake early in the Williams Grove redwood campground and listen to a Varied Thrush calling. The brochure says it sounds like the warning a truck makes when it backs up. I think it could also be a warning to protect the redwoods from global warming. Then a Swainson's Thrush sings. Its ascending two-note phrase evokes joy, not despair, but soon I am back to thinking about redwoods and rising temperatures.

A trip to the redwoods invariably evokes spiritual musing. Even the second growth trees are hundreds of years old, and when they fall, it takes centuries for them to return to the earth. I can feel the green moss on five-hundred year-old furrowed bark and, with the redwood's long-time help, briefly get out of the grief loop.

Home Team Fan

Now that we're unclipping our life line from the mother earth ship, and embarking on a journey where the air quality won't sustain us, how long will we be able to hold our breath while the planet burns and floods? We need to root more right here, right now.

> the shell
> of a rusted car
> in a ditch
> if only we would stop
> abandoning ourselves

Game Of The Century

Oceans will continue to warm and droughts will continue to spread. We keep cheering for the government-industrial complex to go on a solution spree, but their two-hundred-year-old team, saddled with entrenched ideas about what is profitable, is no longer nimble and can't keep up.

Some say that, since we pay money to support the teams, we—the spectators—are also in the game, and should have a say in future decisions.

Too bad we're not all on the same team.

>   swifts scythe
>   the blue between the green
>   at the undammed river
>   no winning
>   no losing

Fight, Flight, Freeze, Fawn

Rivers flood in Europe, people die, and a leader opines, "Climate change is not a future disaster. It's here." Glad forty years of scientific predictions have finally made it into an elected official's speech, but loud declarations without policy change won't help.

Today, I'm losing equanimity. The creatures who depend on us haunt me. The young people haunt me. Do something? Realize the sanctity of all life is aspirational?

> blue sky
> green live oak
> brown dead pines
> I watch the forest fall
> in slow motion

Unenlightened

Before the cataclysms, we worked, hiked, smooched, and ignored the scientific evidence. After the cataclysms, we worked with masks on, stayed inside, smooched desperately, and asked why we hadn't listened.

please help save native trout
keep dogs out of the water
the stream dry now
a river otter?
in that rock crevice?

Anadromous Dreaming

Driest summer in California since measurements began in 1895. Fresh water shortages predicted by 2050. When even our most massive reservoirs have sunk to "historically low levels," will there be any fish left for the dams to kill? Should dystopian climate-future novels be reclassified as non-fiction?

> wild king salmon
> forty-five dollars a pound . . .
> when water's rationed
> and we have to stand in line
> money won't help

911

Without the government's help, we're helpless to halt the climate express, but too many people don't want too much government intervention, because they fear the government will take away their freedoms. Yet the government isn't a predatory zombie, and individual freedom isn't an absolute right. Governments try to balance individual freedom with societal obligation. Governments pass laws that allow us to live together. When they work.

freeze forecast
I refill the hummingbird feeder
torpor only helps
if there's food
in the morning

Gallows Humor

It will be easier to see wildlife as the habitat shrinks, because they will only be able to survive in the small parks we preserve for them. Managed care for all. Yes, there will be entrance fees.

Polar snorkeling. No need to wear a wet suit.

> that night a warbler
> —in color—
> daytime observations
> used to be more common
> than dream birds

Too Many Pieces?

The cracked shapes in the path are a sun-dried puzzle with a trillion pieces, each a shade of brown or gray. We could put the earth back together, but we'd have to look closely at whatever we pick up, which might be too far outside the box for us.

> a bench
> and deer tracks
> at the muddied creek
> could be a diorama
> for future generations

Being Here

We are all limited in our individual ability to significantly lessen the climate catastrophe, but I am also limited in my ability to accept that we have limits. I keep getting stuck between despondency and fury: if-we-can't-do-a-lot-better-soon, every biological kingdom is going to be so much worse off.

I know. I know. No matter what humans do, the earth will keep going, and the destruction we cause is just part of our planet's life cycle. But with great power comes great responsibility, and our governments and businesses aren't there yet.

after the storm
a dead hummingbird
on our porch
I didn't want to pick it up
then didn't want to put it down

Pre-TSD

Fires make me think of fawns.

> back country blaze
> in a forest I'd hoped
> to hike with my daughter
> no one wants to camp
> with charred trees

There will be more fires. Pre-traumatic stress disorder—worrying about highly probable, devastating events which, when they occur, will be worse than we can imagine—is not covered by insurance, and endless group therapy would be the only effective treatment.

Floods make me think of shorebirds.

> the sandpiper flock
> disappears in the sun
> and reappears
> when it changes direction
> I watch

Music Lesson

The philosopher asked what life would be like if we knew we were the last ones. Melancholic? Shame-filled? Certainly not ebullient. It turns out we need the people who have not yet been born. Not sure he included songbirds in this thought problem.

silent-spring canyon
no songs to quiet
my mind-screech
I play the bird app
and remember

Scared Straight

woodland bird walk
hearing aides turned up
still no song
is this silence
an indeterminate sentence?

Climate-fiction. In the beginning, a human-driven heat disaster. In the middle, the characters respond. The end? Either hopeful, to inspire us, or devastating, to horrify us to do better.

scatter my ashes
at Snag Lake meadow . . .
since we've burned
the whole forest now
just add me to the char

The elusive Bewick's wren
of Snag Lake

We Can Do It If We Really Want?

watching a friend
look at a pelican
she no longer recognizes . . .
when birds are gone
they will only be names

Three billion birds lost in North America over the past fifty years. No use looking for them. They're gone. But waterfowl are still here. We gave them what they needed most —our money for habitat—and they multiplied. Forest birds, grassland birds, sea birds, wetland birds: the ornithologist said they wouldn't disappear, either, if we did the same for them.

a hummingbird
on a branch in the rain
I won't know
it's my last one
until it's gone

Caretaker

my friend sees
a wren at her feeder
after it flies
she asks
if we've seen one

Unproven memory-improvement medications with potential side effects will not slow her descent into wonder.

The earth's not in hospice yet, either, but we could slow *its* progressive disease, if we listened to our palliative care team.

hot again
not even a trill
remembering
what we've lost
would help

Lifeline Or Thin Thread?

We invaded—land, sea, air—and the earth couldn't defend itself. Will we keep pillaging until nothing we want is left? It's hard to accept that we could have tried harder and didn't.

Children are too young to grieve the end of an earth they never got to know.

> micro-plastic particles
> in deep ocean sediment
> my granddaughter says
> *Mom said mushrooms*
> *can eat plastic*

Low Probability Events Do Occur

If only cognitive dissonance was the name of a rock band we outgrew after adolescence but, no, it's a genetic defect. Too many of us lack the ability to process information accurately. Now that we've opened the Internet supermarket, where the price of false news is always discounted for quick sale, it's even harder for us to think our way out of the paper bag we've packed ourselves into. And the climate keeps climbing. I'm not usually a follow-the-leader type guy, but maybe a charismatic woman scientist, who also played guitar and did magic tricks, could get us all to buy into a climate malfeasance rehab program.

in a hollow tree
battery candles flicker
around a small fluffy dog
yes, peace with the earth now
please

We take a short backpack in the Sierra. While a not-yet fledged finch calls for food from a short pine, my twelve-year-old granddaughter binds twigs together with penstemon and makes a small raft that she launches in the lake.

Wind, push it to the far shore.

I take a picture.

Remember this.

And I do, in that hazy way some memories are, as she opens the front door every day before eighth-grade middle school for a brown butter scrambled egg breakfast, almost two years later.

Remember this.

She puts her ear buds in and leaves to meet her friend before the first class. Skipping past the thought that if I could live to be a hundred, I could see the adult she will become—and how the climate crash will affect her—I make a note to buy more eggs.

Attention, Please

Lost Bird: Reward

Mid-1950s, snow on the ground, and one morning a flock of Evening Grosbeaks in our backyard. The bird book promised warblers in spring. Back then, climate change was for geologists, extinction for dinosaurs.

> the global thermometer
> cardinal red
> we're goldfinch
> so pleased with our song
> we can't stop

Money, fittest of all survivors, always flies. The oil barons could leave some in the ground, but depending on alpha predators to nurture their prey for the common good is a bad bet. Still, I've got to put my chips down . . . on green

> old jigsaw puzzle
> a robin hidden
> in a leafed-out oak
> I must keep looking
> for the lost piece

BLACKBURNIAN WARBLER

Homework

The author beseeched: we're not separate from nature. If the forests, oceans, and deserts are besieged, we're besieged. Nurture nature, nurture ourselves. Do something to help.

> Sierra forest
> beetle-browned
> and silent
> we could plant more pines . . .
> would they die, too?

Indigenous people lived with nature. "Civilized" people not so much. If we stopped attacking the earth a hundred years from now, would we start caring for it like our child? For now, can we proceed with equanimity and compassion despite ongoing cataclysms? Take the long view? Focus on what we can do?

> granddaughter
> growing a plant jungle
> in her room
> *I'm improving air quality*
> twelve-year-old activist

Fixer-Upper

a raven hides
the rest of the gull chick
in the ice plant cliff
we're the predators who prey
on our own children's future

But if we could accept that our disruptive desires aren't
obligatory . . .

first rains green the hills
a flock lands and feeds
our makeover
of the earth
doesn't have to be permanent

And if we could watch the campfire, pulsating red-orange as the
wood gives up its centuries for our warmth, and see it as a gift . . .

a returning swallow
perches
on a chartreuse-mossed oak
this could be my home
if I widened my gaze

Assessment

So many of us are online, destroying the earth with our credit cards.

> a stranger in line says
> *the earth will survive*
> *just not sure about people—*
> he's searching for comfort
> too

Can't be hopeful; too naive. What's gone isn't coming back.

> billions of years
> from jelly fish
> to us
> no speed bumps
> on our dead-end descent

Can't be hopeless; too dispiriting. Need to be more present.

> find a tree
> beckoningly blossoming
> or bare-branched
> sketch
> listen

Showing Up

fire and smoke
Mount Lassen closed
all those birds
we watched for forty years . . .
did they fly fast enough?

Our ardent wish is to find the wisdom hidden within ourselves to live here in harmony with all the other glories of evolution, but wishes don't pay bills, and unless we ignore all the evidence, undeniably showing we can't live within our earth-bound means, the bill we owe the earth is beyond our ability to make our governments pay, and our individual bank accounts are insufficient. What can we do, beyond raging or clinging to hope, neither of which will stop our species-centered, self-centered rampage through the biosphere?

winter solstice
a crow silhouettes
against the pink dawn
today more light
can be a start

Attention, Please

The spiritual teachers tell me to let go of the outcome. Be present.

> the fragrant iris
> is blooming in our garden
> again
> I go out
> just to inhale

But if the earth's future is unimaginable loss . . .

> my granddaughter's growing
> —vegetables, too—
> and learning earth science
> if only she could plant
> some magic beans

Our teachers now are flowers and climatologists as we plummet.

> those swallows long ago
> fluttering over the gravel road
> where a car killed
> one of their swoop
> now I see they were us

I can close my eyes and see the Short-eared Owl perched on the standing four-foot, broken-off tree trunk in the middle of the meadow as twilight fades to night. Then it's another year, and I see the full-moon-lit meadow, where magic is afoot and anything is possible.

I've spent six months here, over a forty-year period, backpack camping at Snag Lake. The tiny lodgepole pines have advanced on the meadow from the forest, and then have died when a heavy snow-melt year submerged the meadow in two feet of water. I've seen common birds, rare birds, and once, 300 migrating Rufous Hummingbirds.

Last summer the online map showed that the Dixie fire had burned the entire eastern half of Lassen Volcanic National Park. The forest is not green there anymore. Is the meadow now blackened? Next summer, I'll hike back and see if the fire might have missed a small grove here-and-there. I'll see what isn't there anymore. I'll keep my eyes open.

Aah, Green

True Selves?

Solving the climate crisis would be an inner hero's journey. Instead of going on a quest, we'd cross the threshold of the familiar, accept limitations, and heal the earth by looking and listening.

only June
the park creek
a series of pools
our story could be
we finally stopped

Long View/Short View

bay-oak woodland
trying to see
all the shades of green
time slows down
—we're born for this too

So many casualties in our three-hundred-year assault on the earth. Hard to be compassionate about what we've done and are still doing, but one day our planted-sapling peace offerings might shade more than an armistice.

juncos feeding
I veer off the trail
so they won't fly
research shows helping others
helps us, too

Let Us Breathe

a sparrow bathes
in a small mud puddle
I see every bird
as a possible
climate casualty

We need to get back to green, but green is not a primary color. We have to mix yellow-petaled hope with blue ache to connect with a perennial future

A green political party hasn't been enough, but is a new green creed coalescing right now? In the future, will people look back and see this as the time when we all began to green again, when the wisdom of indigenous, seventh generation peoples became our sacred texts? We truncated our vision, but ant-to-mushroom-to zooplankton, will all welcome us prodigal daughters and sons as we return to their fold?

fall forest quiet
a flicker disappears
oak by oak
is the only way back
when we're ready

Aah, green.

Afterword

I wrote most of these pieces between 2019-2021. The news continues to report multiple initiatives that aim to develop sustainable, affordable, scalable ways to lessen greenhouse gas emissions (electrify transportation, increase energy and battery storage, reduce methane leaks) and remove greenhouse gases from the atmosphere (plant more trees, sequester more carbon dioxide and methane). We also continue to hear how individual choices can reduce our greenhouse gas emissions (go solar, drive less, fly less, eat less beef).

We need multiple solutions to the climate crisis, of course, and all our current efforts will help. Will they eventually lead to a change in the zeitgeist, so that we actually, equitably implement a society-wide use-less-non-renewable energy approach (or accept the financial cost and meltdown risk of more nuclear power plants) to get us where we need to go—for ourselves and all the other life on the planet? All those who follow us will know.

David C. Rice
Berkeley, California
July 2022

Alternate Ending?

the bird-willow
two-foot burnt limbs now
and six-inch new growth
it knows
how to reconnect

The US climate bill is a road map toward our let's-not-roast/drown/flood-the-earth destination, and the California bill outlawing sales of new gas-powered cars in 2035 is an off ramp from the no-limits super highway we've been traveling. I like hoopla and celebration as much as anyone, but our ability to deceive ourselves that we are now giant-stepping away from the climate-change crash site is impressive. The Climate Action Tracker website now gives the US an overall rating of "insufficient" toward reaching the goal of keeping the world's temperature rise under three degrees Celsius.

We need to keep going, and we have a long way to go.

blackened bark
needleless
silent
the forest will green again . . .
if we want it enough

Publication Credits

(Some in a slightly different form.)

Assessment—*California Quarterly*
Attention, Please—*Ribbons*
Be Here Now . . . and Then—*red lights* (tanka only)
Being Here—*HWUP!* (tanka only)
Beneficiaries?—*Contemporary Haibun Online*
Connundrum—*red lights* (tanka only)
Fixer-Upper—*Contemporary Haibun Online*
Homework—*Ribbons*
Just Human—*International Tanka*
Let Us Breathe—*Drifting Sands Haibun*
Long View/Short View—*red lights* (first tanka only)
Lost Bird: Reward—*MacQueen's Quinterly*
Lost and Found?—*Tanka 2020* (tanka only)
Low Probability Events Do Occur—*Contemporary Haibun Online*
Mandatory Mediation—*Ribbons*
Music Lesson—*International Tanka*
Next Court Date in Six Months— *MacQueen's Quinterly*
Not on the Wagon Yet— *TSA Member Anthology*
Not Too Big To Fail—*Contemporary Haibun Online*
Pre-TSD—*Kokako*
Range Expansion—*red lights* (tanka only)
Scared Straight—*Bear Creek Haiku* (tanka only)
Showing Up—Fujisan Taisho Award 2021; 1st tanka
Showing Up—*Ribbons* (second tanka)
True Selves?—GUSTS (tanka only)
Tug of War—*red lights* (tanka only)
Unlikely, But—*Bear Creek Haiku*
Was It Just Too Hard to Stop?—*Human/Kind*
We Can Do It If We Really Want?—*red lights* 2nd tanka
Where We're Going—*Ribbons*

Art Work—Tex Buss

Front Cover: Delivery, Oil on Board, 30"x21"

Blackburnian Warbler, Watercolor on paper, 9"x12"

California Quail, Watercolor on Paper, 12"x16",Detail of "Point Reyes Bird Sheet"

Cedar Waxwing, Watercolor on paper, 9"x12"

Chestnut-backed Chickadees, Watercolor on paper, 9"x12"

Hooded Oriole, Watercolor on paper, 9"x12"

Northern Flicker, Watercolor on Paper, 12"x16",Detail of "San Francisco Bird Sheet"

Spotted Towhee, Watercolor on Paper, 12"x16",Detail of "Point Reyes Bird Sheet"

Townsend's Warbler, Watercolor on paper, 9"x12"

Tree Swallow, Watercolor on paper, 9"x12"

Acknowledgments

My wife, Carol Shattuck-Rice, was the first reader of these pieces, and she never hesitated to tell me I needed to "keep working." My friend, Autumn Noelle Hall, a tanka poet, read the first draft and helped me smooth out many rough edges. My daughter, Amanda Abarbanel-Rice read a revised version and told me I needed to re-arrange the order, re-name the sections, and cut duplicates. She was right. Finally, Edith Friedman, a poet and friend of my daughter's, read the "final" version and generously gave me detailed edits, all of which improved the manuscript.

Jacqueline Stuber designed the covers.

Thank you!

I would also like to thank the editors who published some of these pieces in little magazines and online journals.

David C. Rice attended Phillips Exeter Academy, Harvard University, and the University of California, Berkeley, and has worked as a clinical psychologist for fifty years. He has been writing tanka for thirty-plus years, was the editor of the Tanka Society of America's triannual journal from 2012-2019, and has written six books of tanka—four with other poets/artists—as well as a book about the attractions of birding.

—⚬⚬⚬—

Tex Buss began studying painting at the School of Visual Arts, New York. From there her craft took her in various directions, including an ongoing career in tattooing at Red Kestrel Tattoo, and oil painting with a heavy focus on figurative work. She also paints bird and nature-focused watercolors. She is based in San Francisco, where she has shown extensively in galleries.

To see the latest out of her studio, connect with her on Instagram @authentictattoo or on Facebook, Red Kestrel Tattoo. WEBSITE: bussfineart.com